Introduction

Every mother wants to create a room for her child that fosters imagination, growth and wonder. In this book, I'll show you how to create an atmosphere where your child will want to play for hours. Stitch up the Jungle Fun series, and your child or grandchild can go on a safari and explore the far reaches of the jungle. Or stitch up the Under the Sea series and watch your child's imagination soar as he or she dives into the depths of the sea in a submarine.

And don't forget about the monsters—and I don't mean the scary ones under the bed! These monsters are huggable, lovable and will make you laugh as they give a warm fuzzy feeling to everyone they meet. Their bright smiles and goofy faces will help your child see monsters in a whole new light.

No matter which appliqué theme you choose from this book, your child will have hours of fun with their new character friends.

Need a special gift for a baby shower? Stitch up one of the wall hangings and give it to the new parents, or stitch a small quilt to welcome the new baby home. Either way, the gift will be treasured for a lifetime.

The possibilities are endless with these simple and fun appliquéd creatures. Don't stop with these ideas; let your creative juices flow and add these appliqués to backpacks, bath towels, totes, robes and curtains to add more fun and color to your child's room.

Meet the Designer

Margie's mom taught her how to sew when she was a young girl. By the age of 12 she was making her own clothes for school. She made her first quilt at age 14 and still has it today.

In 2008, her love for designing grew and expanded to include quilts. In 2010, Margie started Ribbon Candy Quilt Company. The quilts she designs are for the busy, so her patterns are usually fast and easy. She loves using fusible web appliqué because it's so versatile and allows her to create unique images. Margie is well-known for her *Seasonal Skinnies* patterns, the flagship of her Ribbon Candy Quilt Company.

Margie's designs have been in a number of publications, including *Quiltmaker 100 Blocks, Quiltmaker* magazine, *American Patchwork and Quilting* 2013 calendar, and the book *Springtime in the Rockies,* with more publications on the way.

Margie was born and raised in central California, but has lived in Utah for the past 18 years. She is married, and a mom to five children. When she isn't sewing, you can find her enjoying time with her family or indulging in other hobbies, which include reading, baking, scrapbooking and making jewelry.

To see more of Margie's designs, visit Ribbon Candy patterns blog at: http://ribboncandyquilts.blogspot.com/ and "like" her facebook page at: www.facebook.com/RibbonCandyQuiltCompany.

Table of Contents

Jungle Fun Set,
page 6

Under the Sea Set,
page 26

Friendly Monster Set,
page 36

Jungle Fun Bib,
page 13

General Instructions

Common techniques and general instructions used to construct the projects in this book are referred to in the patterns and explained here. Take a moment to become acquainted with these before beginning your projects.

Basic Tools & Supplies
- Sewing machine in good working order
- Good-quality all-purpose thread to match fabrics
- Sharp scissors
- Seam ripper
- Straight pins and hand-sewing needles
- Measuring tools
- Air- or water-soluble marking pen
- Steam iron, ironing board and pressing cloth
- Pattern tracing paper
- Rotary cutter, mat and straightedges
- Serger

All cuts are precise. All seams are ¼ inch unless otherwise stated. All appliqué images are full size and ready to trace onto the fusible webbing.

Embroidery: Embroidered details are used on most projects. Use 3 strands of embroidery floss and knot one end. Use a backstitch on all mouths and a satin stitch for noses or nostrils and irises or pupils (Figure 1).

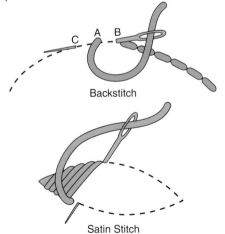

Backstitch

Satin Stitch

Figure 1

Fusible web: Most projects in this book have been constructed with a double-stick fusible web. This product has a pressure-sensitive adhesive on both sides that allows for a temporary hold; there is no pressing until your entire appliqué design is in place

to allow for positioning changes for pieces until you are satisfied with the design.

Medium-weight fusible interfacing: When a very light fabric is fused to a darker or printed fabric, the colors from the underneath layers will probably show through the lighter top layer. To avoid this, you may use a medium-weight fusible interfacing on the wrong side of the lighter appliqué fabric before adding the fusible web and cutting shapes. This extra layer is located between the background and the appliquéd piece in the finished project.

Fusible Appliqué
Follow these general instructions to prepare patterns for appliqué motifs. Refer to the manufacturer's instructions for specifics of fusible web application.

1. If fabrics are prewashed, do not use dryer sheets with fabrics that will be fused.

2. Trace appliqué shapes (shapes are given in reverse for this type of appliqué) on the paper liner. Be sure to leave space in between the images so you can cut them out.

3. Cut out each image ¼ inch from drawn line.

4. Peel off back paper liner and place the sticky side of the fusible web on the wrong side of the fabric. *Note: You will still have the top paper liner that has the drawn image. If a light fabric is being used on top of a dark fabric, apply medium-weight fusible interfacing to the wrong side of these fabrics referring to manufacturer's instructions before applying fusible web.*

5. Using a warm iron, lightly press the fusible web onto the wrong side of the fabric just enough to hold.

6. Let the fabric cool. Transfer all pattern details to fabric using a water-erasable marker.

7. Cut out the images on the drawn line.

8. Trace the complete appliqué motif on a piece of paper with a heavy-line marker. Turn the paper over and trace over the lines to make a right-side-up pattern.

9. Peel off the remaining paper liner and arrange the fabric/fusible web shapes in numerical order, fusible side down on a flat surface, using the traced pattern beneath as a guide for positioning. Move pieces as necessary. **Note:** *The double-stick fusible web allows you to pick up and move pieces around without fusing. You may fuse the shapes together on an appliqué pressing sheet before fusing the entire motif to the background. The whole motif may be picked up off the sheet and moved as one without pieces shifting.*

10. When satisfied with the placement, center the motif image on the background fabric straight and in proper position.

11. Press the image to the background.

12. Hand- or machine-stitch around all raw edges to secure using a zigzag, satin or blanket stitch (Figure 2) or other appliqué or quilting stitch. **Note:** *Without some kind of edge finish or quilting on top of the pieces, the fused shapes may eventually come off.*

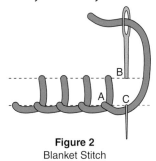

Figure 2
Blanket Stitch

Quilting

Quilting is the process of sewing two layers of fabric together with a layer of batting between. It adds loft while securing the layers.

1. Sandwich the batting piece between the completed top and the prepared backing piece; press out any wrinkles, and pin or baste the layers together.

2. You may quilt in any design you prefer. Several of the projects in this book that use fleece for backing have machine stitching in the ditch of only the seams between pieces, while others have stitching around some of the appliqué shapes. You may add as much quilting as is desired or as recommended by the batting manufacturer.

3. When quilting is complete, trim excess backing and batting even with the edges of the project top to prepare the quilt for binding.

Binding

The projects that require binding as an edge finish in this book use straight-grain binding strips.

To prepare and apply binding, refer to the following instructions.

1. Cut binding strips as directed in individual projects.

2. Join the strips on the short ends with diagonal seams to make one long strip; trim seams to ¼ inch and press open (Figure 3). Cut the starting end on the diagonal and press under ¼ inch.

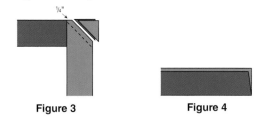

Figure 3   **Figure 4**

3. Fold the strip along the length with wrong sides together and press to make a double-layered strip (Figure 4).

4. Pin the diagonal end of the binding strip to the back-side raw edge of the project at the center of one side, matching raw edges. Begin to stitch binding to project a short distance from a corner of the project using a ¼-inch seam, leaving the diagonal end of binding unstitched. Stop stitching ¼ inch from corner and backstitch (Figure 5).

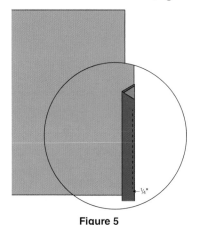

Figure 5

5. Remove quilt from machine and turn. Fold binding up at a 45-degree angle to seam, and then down even with quilt edges forming a pleat at the corner (Figure 6).

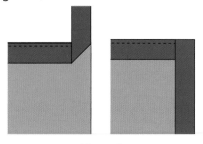

Figure 6

6. Resume stitching at corner, backstitching ¼ inch from corner (Figure 7). Repeat until reaching starting point.

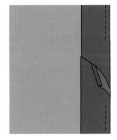

Figure 7   **Figure 8**

7. Cut binding off long enough to tuck inside starting end and complete stitching (Figure 8).

8. Turn binding to quilt front to enclose the seam and stitch in place using a narrow zigzag stitch (Figure 9), mitering each corner (Figure 10).

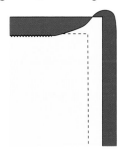

Figure 9   **Figure 10**

Using Low-Pile, Smooth Fleece

There are many trademarked brands of low-pile, smooth fleece. These products are extra soft. They do have a nap and require specific methods for cutting and stitching. The following is a list of hints for use when sewing with fleece.

- Do not use heat on the fleece. It will melt. Instead, if there are wrinkles in the fleece, place the fleece under a towel and press gently on low heat.

- When washing projects that use fleece fabric, wash on a gentle cycle and air-dry.

- Fleece has a nap similar to velvet. Be sure that the nap is facing the direction you want in your finished project before cutting. Pay close attention when cutting if you have multiple pieces from the same fabric and you want the nap to go in the same direction on each piece in the finished project. Run your hand along the length of the fleece. In one direction your hand will be going in the direction of the nap and the fabric will feel smooth; in the other direction you will be going against the nap and the fabric will feel rough. You will be able to feel the difference.

- Some fleece is stable parallel to the selvage but will stretch perpendicular to the selvage (across the width). Remember this when cutting and sewing fleece.

- Prewash any fabrics being used with fleece. The fleece will not shrink, but cotton fabrics used with it may, so the cotton fabrics should be prewashed to prevent problems in the finished project.

- A large amount of lint is created when cutting and sewing fleece pieces. After cutting, shake pieces to remove excess lint or place in a dryer on the air-dry cycle with no heat. Use a vacuum to clean up your sewing area after cutting before proceeding with cutting other fabrics to avoid spreading this excess lint onto your project and work area.

- A 90/14 stretch needle may be used when sewing on fleece.

- All-purpose, 100-percent polyester thread may be used when sewing on fleece.

- Pin every 1–1½ inch to keep the fleece from moving when stitching.

- Test your machine stitching on practice pieces using the fabrics in your project before sewing on your actual project.

- Stitch with the nap rather than against the nap.

- If sewing fleece together with cotton fabric, stitch with the fleece layer down and let the feed dogs guide the fabric.

- Hand basting before machine stitching helps prevent slipping during machine stitching.

- A walking foot may be used to help prevent slipping when machine stitching.

- Use a generous ½-inch seam allowance when stitching because fleece tends to curl when being stitched.

- Clean your machine often when sewing with fleece.

- Use low-loft polyester, 80/20 (cotton/polyester) or prewashed cotton batting if using batting with fleece in a project. ∎

Jungle Fun Set

Decorate with these adorable jungle animals and bring out the adventurer in your child.

Project Note

If you want to make the whole set, a list of materials is given below for all the fabrics needed for the set. Other supplies and notions needed are also listed.

Materials for the Set of 6 Projects

- 1 fat quarter dark aqua tonal cotton fabric
- 44/45-inch-wide cotton fabric:
  - ¼ yard yellow/orange tonal
  - ⅜ yard each brown, cream and dark aqua word prints
  - ½ yard black solid
  - ½ yard each light and dark brown tonals
  - ½ yard medium aqua print
  - ⅝ yard green tonal
  - ¾ yard of each of the following: blue, yellow/orange, green and dark brown polka dots
  - 1 yard orange/yellow tonal
  - 2 yards coordinating stripe (includes binding)
  - 2¼ yards green leaf print
  - 2¾ yards white solid
  - 3½ yards jungle print
  - 3½ yards backing fabric
- 60-inch-wide low-pile, smooth fleece:
  - ⅔ yard blue
  - 1⅔ yards green (quilt backing)

Other Materials

- 1 queen-size quilt batting (80/20 cotton/polyester recommended when used with fleece)
- Coordinating all-purpose thread
- 2 skeins black embroidery floss
- 1 skein each white and blue embroidery floss
- 5½ yards double-stick fusible web
- 1½ yards white medium-weight fusible interfacing
- 1-inch-square hook-and-loop tape
- Basic sewing tools and supplies

Jungle Fun Wall Hanging

Finished Size
Wall Hanging: 18 x 32 inches

Materials
- 1 fat quarter each cotton fabric:
    Green leaf print
    Blue polka dot
    Green tonal
    Yellow/orange polka dot
    Orange/yellow tonal
- 44/45-inch-wide cotton fabric:
    ¼ yard yellow/orange tonal
    ⅓ yard coordinating stripe
    ⅜ yard jungle print
- ⅔ yard blue 60-inch-wide low-pile, smooth fleece
- Batting 20 x 34 inches
- Coordinating all-purpose thread
- Black embroidery floss
- ¾ yard 18-inch-wide double-stick fusible web
- ¾ yard white medium-weight fusible interfacing (optional)
- Basic sewing supplies and equipment

Cutting
Refer to the General Instructions on page 3 for preparing and using patterns from the insert. Transfer all pattern markings to fabric. Use patterns for:

- Small Leaf
- Giraffe Appliqué Motif

From green leaf print:
- Cut six Small Leaf appliqué pieces.

From blue polka dot:
- Cut one 8½ x 18½-inch A rectangle.

From green tonal:
- Cut one 8½ x 18½-inch B rectangle.

From yellow/orange polka dot:
- Cut appliqué motif pieces for Giraffe Spots.

From orange/yellow tonal:
- Cut appliqué motif pieces for Giraffe Hooves, Muzzle and Inner Ears.

From yellow/orange tonal:
- Cut appliqué motif pieces for Giraffe Head/Body and Tail.

From coordinating stripe:
- Cut three 2½-inch by fabric width binding strips.

From jungle print:
- Cut one 8½-inch by fabric width strip. Subcut into two 8½ x 18½-inch C rectangles.

From low-pile, smooth fleece:
- Cut one 20 x 34-inch backing rectangle.

Assembly
Stitch seams with right sides together using a ¼-inch seam allowance and press seams toward darker fabric unless otherwise specified. Refer to General Instructions on page 3 for Fusible Appliqué, Embroidery, Quilting and Binding construction techniques.

1. Arrange and join the A, B and C pieces along the 18½-inch sides to complete the background (Figure 1); press seams away from A.

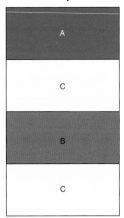

Figure 1

2. Prepare the Giraffe motif for appliqué.

3. Position and fuse the Giraffe motif to the left edge of the background with ear ¾ inch from edge and hooves 1 inch from bottom edge (Figure 2).

Figure 2

4. Arrange and fuse Small Leaf appliqué shapes in place at upper corners ¾ inch from edges referring to the Placement Diagram for positioning.

5. Stitch each appliqué piece in place.

6. Using black embroidery floss, satin-stitch eyes and backstitch mouth and nostrils as marked on pattern for positioning.

7. Quilt and bind to complete the Jungle Fun Wall Hanging.

Jungle Fun Wall Hanging
Placement Diagram 18" x 32"

Jungle Fun Mini Wall Quilts

Finished Sizes
Wall Quilt: 12 x 12 inches

Materials
- Scrap black cotton solid
- 1 fat quarter each cotton fabric:
  Blue, green, dark brown and yellow/orange polka dots
  Orange/yellow, blue and light brown tonals
- 44/45-inch-wide cotton fabric:
  ¼ yard green leaf print
  ⅜ yard white solid
  ½ yard coordinating stripe
  1 yard backing
- 3 (16-inch) squares batting
- Coordinating all-purpose thread
- Black embroidery floss
- ⅝ yard 18-inch-wide double-stick fusible web
- Scrap white medium-weight fusible interfacing (optional)
- Basic sewing supplies and equipment

Cutting
Refer to General Instructions on page 3 for preparing and using patterns. Transfer all pattern markings to fabric. Use medium-size appliqué motifs for:

- Tiger—page 60
- Elephant—page 56
- Monkey—page 63

From scrap black solid:
- Cut appliqué motif piece for Medium Tiger Nose.

From blue polka dot:
- Cut two 2½ x 12½-inch C2 strips.
- Cut appliqué motif pieces for Medium Elephant Ears and Trunk.

From green polka dot:
- Cut two 2½ x 12½-inch C1 strips.

From dark brown polka dot:
- Cut appliqué motif piece for Medium Monkey Head.

From yellow/orange polka dot:
- Cut appliqué motif piece for Medium Tiger Head.

From orange/yellow tonal:
- Cut two 2½ x 12½-inch C3 strips.
- Cut appliqué motif pieces for Medium Tiger Stripes.

From blue tonal:
- Cut appliqué motif piece for Medium Elephant Head.

From light brown tonal:
- Cut appliqué motif pieces for Medium Monkey Face and Muzzle.

From green leaf print:
- Cut two 2½-inch by fabric width strips. Subcut into six 2½ x 8½-inch B strips.

From white solid:
- Cut one 8½-inch by fabric width strip. Subcut into three 8½-inch A squares.
- Cut appliqué motif pieces for Medium Elephant Tusks 1 and 2, and Medium Tiger Inner Ears 1 and 2.

From coordinating stripe:
- Cut five 2¼-inch by fabric width binding strips.

From backing:
- Cut two 16-inch by fabric width strips. Subcut into three 16½-inch backing squares.

Assembly

Stitch right sides together using a ¼-inch seam allowance unless otherwise specified. Refer to General Instructions on page 3 for Fusible Appliqué, Embroidery, Quilting and Binding construction techniques.

1. Prepare the medium-size appliqué motifs for the Tiger, Elephant and Monkey.

2. Center one appliqué motif on each A square and stitch in place in numerical order using a machine blanket stitch and matching thread.

3. Using black embroidery floss, backstitch mouths, and satin-stitch eyes and nostrils where indicated on motifs.

4. Sew B strips to the top and bottom and C1 strips to opposite sides of the appliquéd Tiger square to complete the pieced Tiger top (Figure 1); press.

Figure 1

5. Repeat step 1 with B and C2 strips on the appliquéd Monkey square to complete the pieced Monkey top (Figure 2); press.

Figure 2

6. Repeat step 1 with B and C3 strips on the appliquéd Elephant square to complete the pieced Elephant top (Figure 3); press.

Figure 3

7. Quilt as desired and bind to complete the three Mini Wall Quilts.

Tiger Mini Wall Quilt
Placement Diagram 12" x 12"

Monkey Mini Wall Quilt
Placement Diagram 12" x 12"

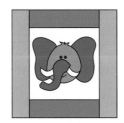

Elephant Mini Wall Quilt
Placement Diagram 12" x 12"

Jungle Fun Bib

Finished Size
Bib: 10¾ x 13½ inches

Materials
- Cotton scraps:
  Blue polka dot
  Blue tonal
  White solid
- 1 fat quarter each cotton fabric:
  Green leaf print
  Cream word print
- Batting 12 x 14½ inches
- Coordinating all-purpose thread
- Black embroidery floss
- 1-inch-square hook-and-loop tape
- 2 (12 x 9-inch) sheets double-stick fusible web
- Scrap white medium-weight fusible interfacing (optional)
- Basic sewing supplies and equipment

Cutting
Refer to the General Instructions on page 3 for preparing and using patterns. Transfer all pattern markings to fabric. Use patterns for:

- Jungle Fun Bib—pattern insert
- Medium Elephant Appliqué Motif—page 56

From scraps:
- Cut appliqué pieces as per Medium Elephant pattern.

From green leaf print:
- Cut one Bib front.

From cream word print:
- Cut one Bib backing.

From batting:
- Cut one Bib piece.

Assembly
Stitch right sides together using a ¼-inch seam allowance unless otherwise specified. Refer to the General Instructions on page 3 for Fusible Appliqué and Embroidery construction techniques.

1. Prepare the Medium Elephant motif for appliqué.

2. Center and fuse the prepared Medium Elephant motif to the Bib front, referring to the Placement diagram for positioning.

3. Stitch appliqué pieces in place.

4. Using black embroidery floss, backstitch mouths and satin-stitch eyes where indicated on appliqué motif.

5. Place the appliquéd bib front and back right sides together matching raw edges. Place the batting piece on top. Pin layers together at edges.

6. Stitch all around the outer edges of the pinned layers, leaving a 3-inch opening on one side (Figure 1).

Figure 1

7. Trim batting close to seam and clip into curves (Figure 2).

Figure 2

8. Turn right side out through opening, using your finger to push out seams; press flat at seam edges.

9. Turn in seam allowance at opening edges (Figure 3); pin closed.

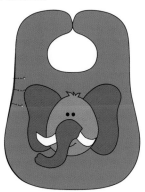

Figure 3

10. Topstitch ⅛ inch from edge all around, closing the opening at the same time (Figure 4).

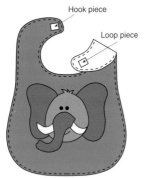

Figure 4

11. Stitch the loop side of tape on the backing side of one neck end and the hook side of tape on the front side of the opposite neck end to finish (Figure 5).

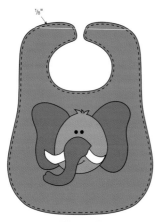

Figure 5

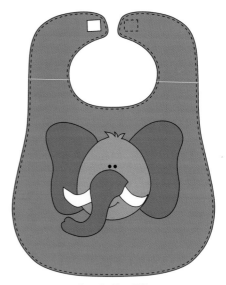

Jungle Fun Bib
Placement Diagram 10¾" x 13½"

Jungle Fun Pillowcase

Finished Size
Pillowcase: Approximately 32¼ x 20¾ inches

Materials
- Cotton scraps:
    Blue, green and dark brown polka dots
    Blue, green and light brown tonals
    44/45-inch-wide cotton fabric:
    ¼ yard coordinating stripe
    ½ yard white solid
    ⅞ yard jungle print
- Coordinating all-purpose thread
- Black embroidery floss
- ½ yard 18-inch-wide double-stick fusible web
- Basic sewing supplies and equipment

Cutting
Refer to General Instructions on page 3 for preparing and using patterns from the insert. Transfer all pattern markings to fabric. Use small-size appliqué motifs for:

- Hippopotamus
- Monkey
- Rhinoceros

From blue polka dot:
- Cut appliqué motif piece for Small Hippopotamus Muzzle.

From green polka dot:
- Cut appliqué motif pieces for Small Rhinoceros Horn and Inner Ear.

From dark brown polka dot:
- Cut appliqué motif piece for Small Monkey Head.

From blue tonal:
- Cut appliqué motif piece for Small Hippopotamus Head.

From green tonal:
- Cut appliqué motif piece for Small Rhinoceros Head.

From light brown tonal:
- Cut appliqué motif pieces for Small Monkey Face and Muzzle.

From coordinating stripe:
- Cut one 3 x 42-inch B strip.

From white solid:
- Cut one 12 x 42-inch C strip.

From jungle print:
- Cut one 27 x 42-inch A strip.

Assembly

Stitch right sides together using a ¼-inch seam allowance unless otherwise specified. Refer to General Instructions on page 3 for Fusible Appliqué and Embroidery construction techniques.

1. Prepare the small-size appliqué motifs for the Rhinoceros, Hippopotamus and Monkey.

2. Fold the C strip in half along length with wrong sides together to make a 6 x 42-inch strip; fold in half across width to make a four-layered 6 x 21-inch strip and press to form creases (Figure 1).

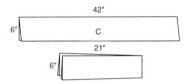

Figure 1

3. Unfold the C strip and lay flat with right side up. Arrange the appliqué motifs within the creased lines on the top half of the left end of the strip (Figure 2).

Figure 2

4. When satisfied with positioning of motifs, fuse pieces in place.

5. Stitch pieces in place in numerical order using a machine blanket stitch and matching thread.

6. Using black embroidery floss, backstitch mouths and satin-stitch eyes and nostrils where indicated on motifs.

7. Fold the B strip in half with wrong sides together along the length to make a double-layered 1½ x 42-inch strip.

8. Pin the folded B strip to one 42-inch edge of the A rectangle, matching raw edges; baste ⅛ inch from edge to hold in place (Figure 3). *Note: The folded edge of the B strip will be free from stitching and loose on top of A.*

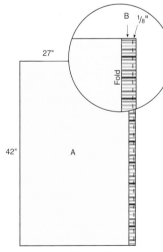

Figure 3

9. Fold under the long plain edge of C ¼ inch and press.

10. Place the C strip right sides together on top of the basted A-B unit, matching raw edges and stitch (Figure 4).

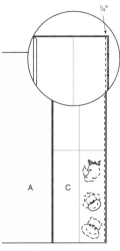

Figure 4

11. Press the C strip to the right side (Figure 5).

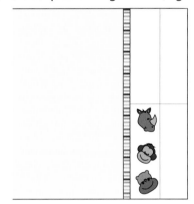

Figure 5

12. Turn the edge of the C strip to the wrong side along the previously creased line to cover and enclose the seam stitched in step 4; pin to hold (Figure 6).

Figure 6

13. Topstitch on the B strip through all layers ⅛ inch from the A-B-C seam, catching the back-side folded edge of C in the stitching (Figure 7).

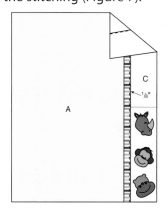

Figure 7

14. Fold the stitched panel in half with right sides together, matching seams between A and B-C, and keeping the folded B strip flat, and pin to hold (Figure 8).

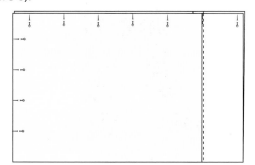

Figure 8

15. Stitch along the raw edge as pinned using a ¼-inch seam allowance. Serge or zigzag raw edges to secure. Turn right side out and press edges to use.

Making a French Seam

If you prefer a stronger seam finish, instead of folding the stitched section right sides together as in step 8, fold it with wrong sides together and stitch. Then turn wrong side out and press. Stitch a second seam ⅜ inch wide to enclose the first seam to make a French seam (Figure 9).

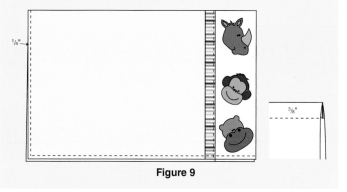

Figure 9

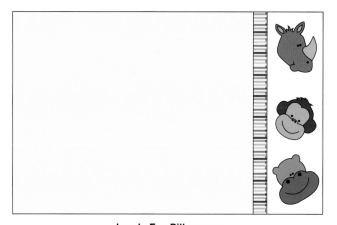

Jungle Fun Pillowcase
Placement Diagram Approximately 32¼" x 20¾"

Jungle Fun Bed Scarf

Finished Sizes
Bed Scarf: 72 x 28 inches
Blocks: 12 x 12 inches and 10 x 12 inches

Materials
- 1 fat quarter each cotton fabric:
  Blue, green, dark brown and yellow/orange polka dots
  Black solid
  Medium aqua print
  Orange/yellow, blue, light brown and dark brown tonals
- 44/45-inch-wide cotton fabric:
  ⅓ yard green tonal
  ½ yard green leaf print
  ⅝ yard coordinating stripe
  1 yard white solid
  1 yard jungle print
  2⅜ yards backing
- Batting 80 x 36 inches
- Coordinating all-purpose thread
- Black and white embroidery floss
- 1½ yards 18-inch-wide double-stick fusible web
- ⅜ yard white medium-weight fusible interfacing (optional)
- Basic sewing supplies and equipment

Cutting
Refer to General Instructions on page 3 for preparing and using patterns from the insert. Transfer all pattern markings to fabric. Use Large and Small Leaf patterns and large-size appliqué motifs for:

- Elephant
- Zebra
- Monkey
- Lion
- Tiger

From blue polka dot:
- Cut one 4½ x 6½-inch D1 rectangle.
- Cut appliqué motif pieces for Large Elephant Ears and Trunk.

From green polka dot:
- Cut one 4½ x 6½-inch D2 rectangle.
- Cut one 2½ x 12½-inch C1 strip.

From dark brown polka dot:
- Cut appliqué motif piece for Large Monkey Head.

From yellow/orange polka dot:
- Cut one 2½ x 12½-inch C6 strip.
- Cut one 4½ x 6½-inch D5 rectangle.
- Cut appliqué motif piece for Large Tiger Head.

From black solid:
- Cut appliqué motif pieces for Large Lion and Large Tiger Noses, and Large Zebra Muzzle, Mane and Stripes.

From medium aqua print:
- Cut one 2½ x 12½-inch C4 strip.
- Cut one 4½ x 6½-inch D6 rectangle.

From orange/yellow tonal:
- Cut one 4½ x 6½-inch D3 rectangle.
- Cut one 2½ x 12½-inch C3 strip.
- Cut appliqué motif pieces for Large Tiger Stripes.

From blue tonal:
- Cut one 2½ x 12½-inch C2 strip.
- Cut appliqué motif piece for Large Elephant Head.

From light brown tonal:
- Cut appliqué motif pieces for Large Monkey Face and Muzzle, and Large Lion Ears and Face.

From dark brown tonal:
- Cut appliqué motif piece for Large Lion Mane.

From green tonal:
- Cut one 1½-inch by fabric width strip.
  Subcut into two 1½ x 16½-inch E strips.
- Cut four 1½-inch by fabric width F strips.

From green leaf print:
- Cut one 4½ x 6½-inch D4 rectangle.
- Cut one 2½ x 12½-inch C5 strip.
- Cut appliqué pieces for 13 Small and 4 Large Leaves.

From coordinating stripe:
- Cut six 2¼-inch by fabric width binding strips.

From white solid:
- Cut two 12½-inch by fabric width strips.
  Subcut into three 12½-inch A squares and two 10½ x 12½-inch B rectangles.
- Cut appliqué motif pieces for Large Zebra Head, Large Elephant Tusks 1 and 2, and Large Tiger Inner Ears 1 and 2.

From jungle print:
- Cut one 5½-inch by fabric width strip.
  Subcut into two 5½ x 18½-inch G strips.
- Cut four 5½-inch by fabric width H strips.

Assembly

Stitch right sides together using a ¼-inch seam allowance unless otherwise specified. Refer to General Instructions on page 3 for Fusible Appliqué, Embroidery, Quilting and Binding construction techniques.

1. Prepare the large-size appliqué motifs for the Tiger, Lion, Elephant, Monkey and Zebra.

2. Select one A square, the Large Tiger motif and two Large Leaves.

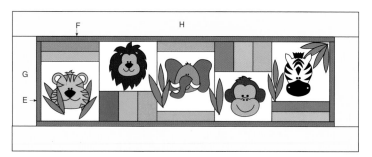

Jungle Fun Bed Scarf
Placement Diagram 72" x 28"

3. Arrange the two Large Leaves on the A square with the Tiger motif centered on A on top of the Large Leaves referring to the pattern and Figure 1 for positioning.

Figure 1

4. When satisfied with positioning of Leaves and Tiger motif, fuse pieces in place.

5. Stitch pieces in place in numerical order using a machine blanket stitch and matching thread.

6. Center and fuse the Large Elephant and Large Zebra motifs on the remaining A squares, and the Large Lion and Large Monkey motifs on the B rectangles, placing one Small Leaf behind the Zebra motif before fusing (Figure 2).

Figure 2

7. Stitch all pieces in place in numerical order using a machine blanket stitch and matching thread.

8. Backstitch mouths and satin-stitch eyes and nostrils where indicated on motifs referring to project photo for color.

9. Sew C1 and then C2 to the top edge of the Tiger block (Figure 3); press seams toward strips.

Figure 3

10. Sew C3 to the top and C4 to the bottom of the Elephant block (Figure 4); press seams toward strips.

Figure 4

11. Sew C5 and then C6 to bottom of the Zebra block (Figure 5); press seams toward strips.

Figure 5

12. Join D1, D2 and D3 on the 6½-inch sides; press. Sew this D unit to the bottom of the Lion block (Figure 6); press seam toward D unit.

Figure 6

13. Repeat step 4 with D4, D5 and D6, and the Monkey block (Figure 7); press seam toward D unit.

Figure 7

14. Join the block units to complete the pieced background referring to the Placement Diagram; press.

15. Arrange, fuse, appliqué and stitch the remaining Leaf shapes on the pieced background, referring to the Placement Diagram for positioning of Leaves.

16. Join the F strips on the short ends to make a long strip; press. Subcut strip into two 1½ x 62½-inch F strips.

17. Sew the E strips to the short ends and F strips to opposite long sides of the pieced center; press.

18. Join the H strips on the short ends to make a long strip; press. Subcut strips into two 5½ x 72½-inch H strips.

19. Sew the G strips to the short ends and H strips to opposite long sides of the pieced center to complete the bed scarf top; press.

20. Quilt as desired and bind to complete the Jungle Fun Bed Scarf.

Adorable Animal Appliqué

Jungle Fun Quilt

Finished Size
Quilt: 48 x 48 inches

Materials
- 1 (10-inch) square each brown and dark aqua word cotton prints
- 1 fat quarter each cotton fabric:
  Blue, green, dark brown and yellow/orange polka dots
  Black solid
  Medium aqua print
  Orange/yellow, green, blue, dark aqua, light brown and dark brown tonals
- 44/45-inch-wide cotton fabric:
  ½ yard coordinating stripe
  ⅔ yard green leaf print
  ¾ yard white solid
  ⅞ yard jungle print
- 1⅔ yards 60-inch-wide green low-pile, smooth fleece
- Batting 56 x 56 inches
- Coordinating all-purpose thread
- Black, white and blue embroidery floss
- 1½ yards 18-inch-wide double-stick fusible web
- Scrap white medium-weight fusible interfacing (optional)
- Basic sewing supplies and equipment

Cutting
Refer to General Instructions on page 3 for preparing and using patterns. Transfer all pattern markings to fabric. Use medium-size appliqué motifs for:

- Elephant—page 56
- Zebra—page 57
- Peacock—page 58
- Lion—page 59
- Tiger—page 60
- Hippopotamus—page 61
- Rhinoceros—page 62
- Monkey—page 63

From all 10-inch squares:
- Trim each 10-inch square to an 8½-inch square for B.

From blue polka dot:
- Cut appliqué motif pieces for Medium Elephant Ears and Trunk, and Medium Hippopotamus Muzzle.

From green polka dot:
- Cut one 8½-inch B square.
- Cut appliqué motif pieces for Medium Rhinoceros Inner Ear and Horn.

From dark brown polka dot:
- Cut appliqué motif piece for Medium Monkey Head.

From yellow/orange polka dot:
- Cut one 8½-inch B square.
- Cut appliqué motif piece for Medium Tiger Head.

From black solid:
- Cut appliqué motif pieces for Medium Lion and Medium Tiger Nose pieces, and Medium Zebra Muzzle, Mane, Inner Ears and Stripes.

From medium aqua print:
- Cut appliqué motif piece for Medium Peacock Feathers.

From orange/yellow tonal:
- Cut one 8½-inch B square.
- Cut appliqué motif pieces for Medium Tiger Stripes and Medium Peacock Feet and Beak.

From green tonal:
- Cut one 8½-inch B square.
- Cut appliqué motif piece for Medium Rhinoceros Head.

From blue tonal:
- Cut one 8½-inch B square.
- Cut appliqué motif pieces for Medium Hippopotamus Head and Medium Elephant Head.

From dark aqua tonal:
- Cut appliqué motif piece for Medium Peacock Body.

From light brown tonal:
- Cut appliqué motif pieces for Medium Monkey Face and Muzzle, and Medium Lion Ears and Face.

From dark brown tonal:
- Cut appliqué motif piece for Medium Lion Mane.

From coordinating stripe:
- Cut five 2½-inch by fabric width binding strips.

From green leaf print:
- Cut one 8½-inch by fabric width strip. Subcut into one 8½-inch B square and four 6½-inch F squares.
- Cut two 2½ x 32½-inch C strips.
- Cut two 2½ x 36½-inch D strips.

From white solid:
- Cut appliqué motif pieces for Medium Zebra Head, Medium Elephant Tusks 1 and 2, Medium Hippopotamus Tooth and Medium Tiger Inner Ears 1 and 2.
- Cut two 8½-inch by fabric width strips. Subcut into eight 8½-inch A squares.

From jungle print:
- Cut four 6½ x 36½-inch E strips.

From low-pile, smooth fleece:
- Cut one 56 x 56-inch backing rectangle.

Assembly

Stitch right sides together using a ¼-inch seam allowance unless otherwise specified. Refer to General Instructions on page 3 for Fusible Appliqué, Embroidery, Quilting and Binding construction techniques.

1. Prepare the medium-size appliqué motifs for the Elephant, Peacock, Zebra, Lion, Tiger, Hippopotamus, Rhinoceros and Monkey.

2. Center one appliqué motif on each A square and stitch in place in numerical order using a machine blanket stitch and matching thread.

3. Backstitch mouths and satin-stitch eyes and nostrils where indicated on patterns and referring to project photo for color.

4. Arrange and join the appliquéd A squares with the B squares in four rows of two appliqué A

squares and two B squares each referring to the Placement Diagram for positioning of blocks and squares; press seams in opposite directions from row to row. **Note:** *Not all appliquéd blocks are in an upright position in the rows on the sample. Note that the rows alternate starting with A squares in one row and B squares in the next row.*

5. Join the rows as arranged and referring to the Placement Diagram to complete the pieced center; press seams in one direction.

6. Sew the C strips to opposite sides and D strips to the top and bottom of the pieced center; press seams toward C and D.

7. Sew E strips to opposite sides; press seams toward E.

8. Sew an F square to each end of each remaining E strip; press. Sew these E-F strips to the top and bottom of the pieced center to complete the quilt top; press seams toward E-F strips.

9. Quilt as desired and bind to complete the Jungle Fun Quilt. ■

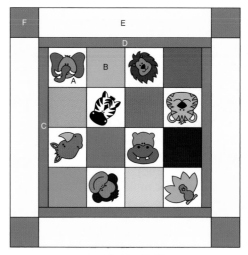

Jungle Fun Quilt
Placement Diagram 48" x 48"

Under the Sea Set

Introduce your child to the wonderful colors
and creatures that live under the sea.

Project Note

If you want to make the whole set, a list of materials
is given below for all the fabrics needed for the set.
Other supplies and notions needed are listed with
the materials for the individual projects.

Materials for the Set of 3 Projects

- Scrap cotton hot pink tonal
- 1 fat quarter white cotton solid
- 1 fat quarter each tonal cotton fabric:
    Yellow
    Light orange
    Orange
    Light green
    Light pink
    Light blue
    Dark rose
    Purple
    Coral
    Tan
    Light aqua
    Dark green
- 44/45-inch-wide cotton fabric:
    ⅓ yard cream tonal
    ⅜ yard light pink tonal
    ½ yard medium green tonal
    1½ yards dark aqua tonal
    2 yards pale blue tonal
    2⅜ yards backing
- 15 x 17-inch rectangle cotton lining (for pillow)
- 60-inch-wide low-pile, smooth fleece:
    Scraps white and dark blue
    1 (12 x 16-inch) rectangle each orange, lime
        green and hot pink
    1 (7-inch) square each yellow and pink
    ⅛ yard medium green
    ½ yard medium blue
    1 yard light blue

Other Materials

- 1 twin-size quilt batting (80/20 cotton/polyester
  recommended when used with fleece)
- 46 x 34-inch rectangle canvas painter's tarp or
  outdoor canvas (rug backing)
- Coordinating all-purpose thread
- 1 skein each black, blue and orange embroidery floss
- 13 (7-inch) lengths various ribbon trims
- Polyester fiberfill
- 2½ yards double-stick fusible web
- ⅛ yard white medium-weight fusible interfacing
  (optional)
- Basic sewing tools and supplies

Under the Sea Jellyfish Pillow

Finished Size
Pillow: 14 x 16 inches

Materials
- Cotton scraps:
  White solid
  Hot pink tonal
- 10-inch square light pink cotton tonal
- 1 fat quarter light aqua cotton tonal
- ½ yard dark aqua 44/45-inch-wide cotton tonal
- 15 x 17-inch rectangle cotton lining
- 15 x 17-inch rectangle cotton batting
- Coordinating all-purpose thread
- Black embroidery floss
- 13 (7-inch) lengths various ribbon trims
- Polyester fiberfill
- 1 sheet double-stick fusible web
- Scrap white medium-weight fusible interfacing
- Basic sewing supplies and equipment

Cutting
Refer to General Instructions on page 3 for preparing and using patterns from the insert. Transfer all pattern markings to fabric. Use Jellyfish appliqué motif.

From white solid scrap:
- Cut appliqué motif piece for Jellyfish Eyes.

From hot pink tonal scrap:
- Cut appliqué motif piece for Jellyfish Bottom.

From light pink tonal:
- Cut appliqué motif piece for Jellyfish Top.

From light aqua tonal:
- Cut one 10½ x 12½-inch A rectangle.

From dark aqua tonal:
- Cut one 14½-inch by fabric width strip.
  Subcut into one 14½ x 16½-inch pillow back and two each 2½ x 12½-inch B strips and 2½ x 14½-inch C strips.

Assembly

Stitch right sides together using a ¼-inch seam allowance unless otherwise specified. Refer to General Instructions on page 3 for Fusible Appliqué and Embroidery construction techniques.

1. Prepare the appliqué motif for the Jellyfish referring to the patterns.

2. Center and pin the appliqué motif ¾ inch down from the top 10½-inch edge of the A rectangle (Figure 1).

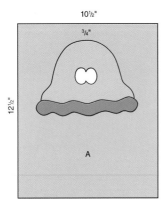

Figure 1

3. Insert and pin the 13 pieces of ribbon trims under the bottom edge of the Jellyfish motif (Figure 2). When satisfied with positioning, fuse the Jellyfish in place over the edges of the ends of the ribbon trim, removing pins as you fuse.

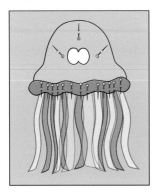

Figure 2

4. Stitch pieces in place in numerical order using a machine blanket stitch and matching thread.

5. Using black embroidery floss, backstitch mouth and satin-stitch eyes referring to the General Instructions on page 3.

6. Sew B strips to opposite sides and C strips to the top and bottom of the appliquéd A rectangle to complete the pillow top (Figure 3); press seams toward B and C strips.

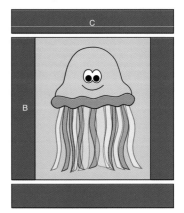

Figure 3

7. Sandwich the batting rectangle between the appliquéd top and the lining rectangle; quilt as desired, being careful not to stitch through the dangling ribbon ends.

8. Trim excess lining and batting even with the appliquéd top edges to complete the pillow top.

9. Place the 14½ x 16½-inch pillow back rectangle right sides together with the pillow top; stitch all around, leaving a 5-inch opening on the bottom edge (Figure 4).

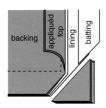

Figure 4

10. Clip corners; trim batting close to seam (Figure 5).

Figure 5

11. Turn the stitched pillow right side out through the opening; poke out the corners and press flat at seams.

12. Insert the polyester fiberfill for desired loft.

13. Turn the opening edges to the inside ¼ inch and hand-stitch the opening closed to finish (Figure 6).

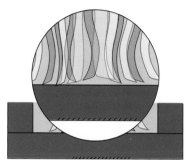

Figure 6

Under the Sea Jellyfish Pillow
Placement Diagram 14" x 16"

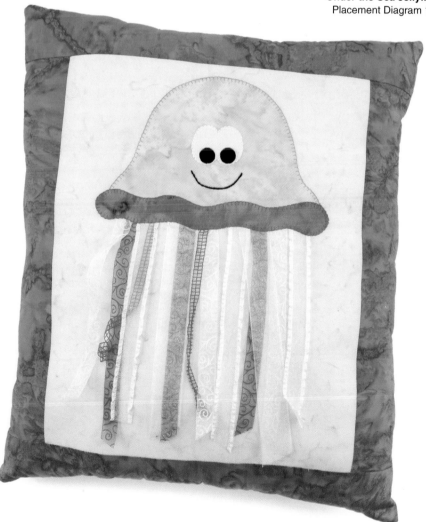

Under the Sea Bed Scarf

Finished Size
Bed Scarf: 70 x 24 inches

Materials
- 1 fat quarter white cotton solid
- 1 fat quarter each cotton tonal fabric:
    Yellow
    Light orange
    Orange
    Light green
    Light pink
    Light blued
    Dark rose
    Purple
    Coral
    Tan
    Dark green
- 44/45-inch-wide cotton fabric:
    ⅓ yard cream tonal
    ½ yard medium green tonal
    ⅞ yard dark aqua tonal
    2 yards pale blue tonal
    2⅜ yards backing
- Batting 78 x 32 inches
- Coordinating all-purpose thread
- Black, blue and orange embroidery floss
- 2 yards 18-inch-wide double-stick fusible web
- ⅛ yard white medium-eight fusible interfacing (optional)
- Basic sewing supplies and equipment

Cutting
Refer to General Instructions on page 3 for preparing and using patterns from the insert. Transfer all pattern markings to fabric. Use appliqué pieces or motifs for:

- Sea Leaf
- 3-Rock Group
- 7-Rock Group
- Octopus
- Dolphin
- Seaweed
- Coral
- Small Fish
- Large and Small Sea Horses
- Large Rock/Scallop Shell/Starfish

From white solid:
- Cut appliqué motif pieces for Dolphin Belly, and Octopus and Small Fish Eyes.

From yellow tonal:
- Cut appliqué motif piece for Small Fish Body.

From light orange tonal:
- Cut appliqué motif pieces for Large and Small Seahorse Bodies, and Scallop Shell.

From orange tonal:
- Cut appliqué motif piece for Small Fish Fins/Tail.

From light green tonal:
- Cut appliqué pieces for Sea Leaves.

From light pink tonal:
- Cut appliqué motif pieces for Small Fish Body, and Dolphin Body and Fin.

From light blue tonal:
- Cut appliqué motif pieces for Small Fish Body.

From dark rose tonal:
- Cut appliqué motif pieces for Small Fish Fins/Tail and Mouths.

From purple tonal:
- Cut appliqué motif piece for Octopus.

From coral tonal:
- Cut appliqué motif pieces for Large and Small Seahorse Manes and Fins, and Coral.

From tan tonal:
• Cut appliqué motif pieces for the 3-Rock, and the 7-Rock Group and Large Rock.

From dark green tonal:
• Cut appliqué piece for Seaweed.

From cream tonal:
• Cut two 3¼-inch by fabric width strips for sand.

From medium green tonal:
• Cut five 2¼-inch by fabric width binding strips.

From dark aqua tonal:
• Cut appliqué motif pieces for Small Fish Fins/Tail and Starfish.
• Cut five 3½-inch by fabric width strips.
   Subcut one strip into two 3½ x 18½-inch B strips. Set aside remaining strips for C.

From pale blue tonal:
• Cut one 18½ x 64½-inch A rectangle along length of fabric.

From backing:
• Cut one 32 x 78-inch backing rectangle.

Assembly

Stitch right sides together using a ¼-inch seam allowance unless otherwise specified. Refer to General Instructions on page 3 for Fusible Appliqué, Embroidery, Quilting and Binding construction techniques.

1. Prepare the appliqué motifs for the 3-Rock and 7-Rock Groups and the Large Rock/Scallop Shell/ Starfish, three Small Fish, Large and Small Sea Horses, Octopus and Dolphin.

2. Join the two 3¼-inch wide cream tonal strips on the short ends to make a long strip; trim to 3¼ x 64½ inches. Draw a pleasing curved line across one long side, making dips no more than 1¾-inch deep to create the bottom sand appliqué piece (Figure 1).

Figure 1

3. Arrange and pin the sand appliqué piece on one long edge of A, matching the straight raw edges.

4. Stitch the sand piece in place along the curved edge using a machine blanket stitch and matching thread. Machine-baste long straight edges and ends in place (Figure 2).

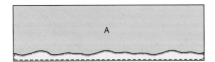
Figure 2

5. Arrange remaining motifs in place on A referring to the Placement Diagram for suggested positioning.

6. Overlap leaf pieces at bottom points with the 3-Rock motif on top (Figure 3).

Figure 3

7. Overlap Seaweed tips and Large and Small Sea Horse motifs (Figure 4).

Figure 4

8. Place the Starfish and Scallop Shell overlapping the Large Rock (Figure 5).

Figure 5

9. When satisfied with placement, fuse all shapes in place.

10. Stitch all pieces in place beginning with the lowest piece in a layered section and using a machine blanket stitch and matching thread.

11. Backstitch Octopus mouth and satin stitch irises using black floss. Satin-stitch irises on the Small Fish and one eye on the Dolphin using blue floss. Satin-stitch eyes and spots on the Large and Small Sea Horses using orange floss.

12. Join the C strips on the short ends to make a long strip; subcut strip into two 3½ x 70½-inch C strips.

13. Sew B strips to opposite short ends and C strips to opposite long edges of the appliquéd center to complete the bed scarf top (Figure 6); press seams toward B and C strips.

Figure 6

14. Quilt as desired and bind to complete the Under the Sea Bed Scarf.

Under the Sea Bed Scarf
Placement Diagram 70" x 24"

Under the Sea Rug

Finished Size
Rug: 40 x 28 inches

Materials
- 60-inch-wide low-pile, smooth fleece:
  Scraps white and dark blue
  1 (12 x 16-inch) rectangle each orange, lime green and hot pink
  1 (7-inch) square each yellow and pink
  1/8 yard medium green
  1/2 yard medium blue
  1 yard light blue
- Coordinating all-purpose thread
- 46 x 34-inch rectangle canvas painter's tarp or outdoor tarp (backing)
- 80/20 batting 46 x 34 inches
- Black fabric marker
- Basic sewing supplies and equipment

Cutting
Refer to General Instructions on page 3 for preparing and using patterns from the insert. Transfer all pattern markings to fabric. Use Under the Sea Rug patterns for:

- Large Fish
- Small, Medium and Large Bubbles

From white:
- Cut Large Fish Eye pieces as per pattern and instructions.

From dark blue:
- Cut Large Fish Iris pieces as per pattern and instructions.

From orange, lime green & hot pink:
- Cut Large Fish Fin/Tail piece from each and Mouth pieces from hot pink as per patterns and instructions.

From yellow & pink:
- Cut Large Fish Body from each as per pattern and instructions.

From medium green:
- Cut two ½ x 60-inch strips.
  Subcut into 10 strips of varying lengths from 5–11 inches for seaweed.

From medium blue:
- Cut three 2 x 60-inch binding strips.
- Cut one Large Fish Body and three each Small, Medium and Large Bubbles as per patterns and instructions.

From light blue:
- Cut one 40 x 28-inch A rectangle for background.

Assembly
Refer to General Instructions on page 3 for Using Low-Pile, Smooth Fleece construction techniques.

1. Trace the Large Fish Fin/Tail, Body and Mouth, Eye and Iris patterns, and the Bubble patterns given in the insert onto pattern tracing paper, reversing one each Body and Fin/Tail patterns. Cut out the paper patterns, leaving a margin around each one. Transfer all information to the paper patterns.

2. Pin each pattern to the wrong side of the appropriate color fleece as directed on patterns and trace around outer edges with a black fabric marker. Remove pattern and cut out pieces on the traced lines.

3. Arrange, layer and pin the Large Fish Fin/Tail pieces, Bodies, Eyes, Irises and Mouth shapes on the A rectangle (Figure 1).

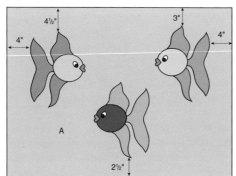

Figure 1

4. Using thread to match fabrics and a close, narrow zigzag stitch, stitch pieces in place in numerical order referring to patterns.

5. Arrange a Large, Medium and Small Bubble circle above the Mouth area of each Fish shape referring to the Placement Diagram for positioning; stitch in place as in step 4.

6. Arrange and pin five seaweed strips in a group, touching bottom of strips together and fanning ends out to create a seaweed group (Figure 2).

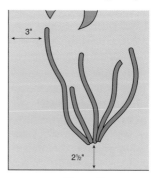

Figure 2

7. When satisfied with positioning, stitch through the center of each strip (Figure 3), reversing stitching at the beginning and end to secure.

Figure 3

8. Repeat to add a second seaweed group.

9. Sandwich the batting between the top of the rug and the canvas backing.

10. Using thread to match fabrics, stitch around the appliqué shapes to hold the layers together.

11. When stitching is complete, trim batting and canvas backing edges even with raw edges of the rug top.

12. Join the three 2-inch-wide binding strips on the short ends with diagonal seams referring to the Binding section of the General Instructions on page 3.

13. Increase machine stitch length to 3.0. Pin and stitch the binding to the canvas backing side of the layered rug using a ½-inch seam allowance, matching raw edges and mitering corners and overlapping at beginning and end, again referring to page 3.

14. Bring the binding strip to the right side of the rug, and sew down over seam, turning the raw edge ½ inch to the wrong side as you stitch (Figure 4) to finish the rug. ■

Under the Sea Rug
Placement Diagram 40" x 28"

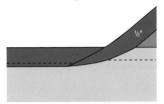

Figure 4

Friendly Monster Set

Not all monsters are scary. These friendly and huggable monsters will bring a smile to your child's face.

Project Note

If you want to make the whole set, a list of materials is given to the right for all the fabrics needed for the set. Other supplies and notions needed are listed with the materials for the individual projects.

Materials for the Set of 4 Projects

- Cotton scraps:
    Yellow/orange polka dot
    Orange stripe
    Blue print
    Medium blue, dark green, yellow and dark
        yellow tonals
- 1 fat quarter each cotton fabric:
    Green polka dot
    Orange dot
    Dark orange tonal
    Light and dark green tonals
- 44/45-inch-wide cotton fabric:
    ½ yard medium green tonal
    ½ yard dark blue print
    1¼ yards coordinating stripe
    1½ yards white solid
    1½ yards medium orange tonal
    1½ yards dark blue polka dot
    1½ yards backing fabric
- 60-inch-wide low-pile, smooth fleece:
    Scraps yellow and orange
    ⅝ yard lime green
    ¾ yard dark blue
    1 yard white

Other Materials

- 30 x 42-inch canvas painter's tarp or outdoor canvas (rug back)
- 1 twin-size quilt batting (80/20 cotton/polyester recommended when used with fleece)
- Coordinating all-purpose thread
- Blue, green and orange embroidery floss
- Polyester fiberfill
- 2 yards 18-inch width double-sided fusible web
- ¼ yard white medium-weight fusible interfacing (optional)
- ¾ yard green jumbo rickrack
- 7 inches blue medium rickrack
- 8 inches green narrow rickrack
- 9 inches ¼-inch-wide blue ribbon
- Pattern paper
- Black fabric marker
- Basic sewing tools and supplies

Friendly Monster Rug

Finished Size
Rug: 36 x 24 inches

Materials
- 60-inch-wide low-pile, smooth fleece:
  - Scraps yellow and orange
  - ⅜ yard lime green
  - ¾ yard dark blue
  - ⅞ yard white
- Coordinating all-purpose thread
- ½ yard green jumbo rickrack
- 30 x 42-inch rectangle canvas painter's tarp or outdoor canvas (backing)
- 80/20 batting 30 x 42 inches
- Black fabric marker
- Basic sewing supplies and equipment

Cutting
Refer to General Instructions on page 3 for preparing and using patterns from the insert. Transfer all pattern markings to fabric. Use Friendly Monster Rug patterns for:

- Iris
- Eyes
- Eyebrow
- Teeth
- Horn and Horn Sections 1, 2 and 3

From yellow scrap:
- Cut Horn Sections 1–3 as per patterns and instructions.

From orange scrap:
- Cut Horn and Teeth pieces as per patterns and instructions.

From lime green:
- Cut two 4½ x 24-inch strips for end zigzag pieces.
- Cut Eyebrow pieces as per pattern and instructions.

From dark blue:
- Cut a 15-inch-diameter circle as per instructions. *Note: You may trace a large mixing bowl or round platter that is close to this size instead of making a pattern.*
- Cut Iris piece as per pattern and instructions.
- Cut three 2 x 60-inch binding strips.

From white:
- Cut a 36 x 24-inch rectangle for background.
- Cut Eyes piece as per pattern and instructions.

Assembly

Refer to General Instructions on page 3 for Using Low-Pile, SmoothFleece construction techniques.

1. Trace the Horn, Horn Sections, Eyebrow, Iris (trace twice to make two templates), Teeth and Eyes onto pattern tracing paper; flip Horn, Horn Sections and Eyebrow to trace for reverse templates. Trace an approximately 15-inch circle onto the pattern tracing paper using a round object close to that size. Cut out the paper patterns, leaving a margin around each one. Transfer all information to the paper patterns.

2. Pin each pattern to the wrong side of the appropriate color fleece as directed on patterns. Pin the 15-inch circle on dark blue. Trace around outer edges with a black fabric marker. Remove patterns and cut out pieces on the traced lines.

3. Arrange and pin the Horn Sections on the Horn pieces referring to pattern for positioning (Figure 1).

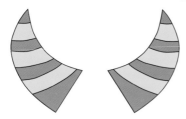

Figure 1

4. Using thread to match the Horn Sections and a close, narrow zigzag stitch, sew sections to the Horn pieces.

5. Repeat steps 3 and 4 with each Iris on the Eyes piece (Figure 2).

Figure 2

6. Cut a 14-inch piece of green rickrack. Arrange in a smile shape 2½ inches from the edge of the 15-inch circle; pin Teeth piece under the left end ½ inch from end of rickrack (Figure 3). Straight-stitch the rickrack and bottom edge of Teeth in place using matching thread.

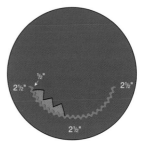

Figure 3

7. Stitch remaining edges of Teeth in place as in step 4.

8. Arrange and pin the Eyes/Iris unit and Eyebrows on the circle and stitch in place as in step 4 (Figure 4).

Figure 4

9. Center and pin the appliquéd circle on the 36 x 24-inch white background rectangle. Insert the appliquéd Horn pieces under top edges of the circle with bottom edges of horns above ends of smile line on outer edges referring to Figure 5 and project photo for positioning. Stitch circle and horns in place as in step 4.

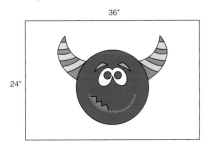

36"

24"

Figure 5

10. Measure and mark a zigzag pattern on the wrong side of the lime green strips (Figure 6). Cut out zigzag pieces on the marked lines.

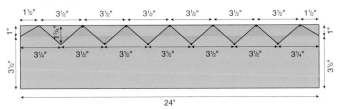

1½"   3½"   3½"   3½"   3½"   3½"   3½"   1½"

1"   ¾"   1"

3½"   3¼"   3½"   3½"   3½"   3½"   3½"   3¼"   3½"

24"

Figure 6

11. Pin and stitch a zigzag piece along each end of the white background to complete the top of the rug.

12. Sandwich the batting between the top of the rug and the canvas backing; pin or baste layers together.

13. Using thread to match fabrics, stitch around the appliqué shapes to hold the layers together.

14. When stitching is complete, trim batting and canvas backing edges even with raw edges of the rug top.

15. Join the three 2-inch-wide binding strips on the short ends with diagonal seams.

16. Increase machine stitch length to 3.0. Pin and stitch the binding to the canvas backing side of the layered rug using a ½-inch seam allowance, matching raw edges and mitering corners and overlapping at beginning and end.

17. Bring the binding strip to the right side of the rug, and sew down over seam, turning the raw edge ½ inch to the wrong side as you stitch (Figure 7) to finish the rug.

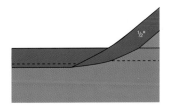

½"

Figure 7

Friendly Monster Rug
Placement Diagram 36" x 24"

Friendly Monster Huggy Pillow

Finished Size
Pillow: 10 x 12 inches, excluding arms

Materials
- Cotton scraps:
    - Dark blue polka dot
    - Dark orange dot
- 1 fat quarter dark blue cotton print
- 44/45-inch-wide cotton fabric:
    - ⅜ yard coordinating stripe
    - ⅜ yard medium green tonal
    - ⅜ yard white solid
- ¼ yard lime green 60-inch-wide low-pile, smooth fleece
- Coordinating all-purpose thread
- Polyester fiberfill
- ¾ yard 18-inch-wide double-stick fusible web
- Scrap white medium-weight fusible interfacing (optional)
- Basic sewing supplies and equipment

Cutting
Refer to General Instructions on page 3 for preparing and using patterns from insert. Transfer all pattern markings to fabric. Use the Huggy Monster appliqué motif.

From dark blue polka dot:
- Cut appliqué motif piece for Monster Iris.

From orange dot:
- Cut appliqué motif piece for Monster Mouth.

From dark blue print:
- Cut appliqué motif piece for Monster Hair.

From coordinating stripe:
- Cut one 10½ x 12½-inch backing rectangle.

From medium green tonal:
- Cut appliqué motif piece for Monster Head.

From white solid:
- Cut one 10½ x 12½-inch A rectangle.
- Cut appliqué motif pieces for Monster Eye and Tooth.

From lime green low-pile, smooth fleece:
- Cut four Monster Arm pieces, reversing 2.

Assembly

Stitch right sides together using a ¼-inch seam allowance unless otherwise specified. Refer to General Instructions on page 3 for Fusible Appliqué and Embroidery construction techniques.

1. Prepare the appliqué motif for the Huggy Monster.

2. Center and fuse the appliqué motif on the A rectangle (Figure 1).

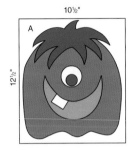

10½"

12½"

A

Figure 1

3. Stitch pieces in place in numerical order using a machine blanket stitch and matching thread.

4. Place an arm and a reverse arm piece wrong sides together to make an arm with a front and back; using a long zigzag stitch, sew ⅛ inch from edge all around to hold the layers together (Figure 2). Repeat with the second set of arm pieces to complete two arms.

⅛"

Figure 2

5. Pin an arm (with thumb side up) to opposite sides of the appliquéd A rectangle 3¼ inches up from the bottom edge. Machine-baste in place ⅛ inch from edge (Figure 3).

⅛"

3¼" 3¼"

Figure 3

6. Matching raw edges, place the appliquéd A rectangle right sides together with the backing rectangle, keeping arms inside between the layers; stitch all around, leaving a 5-inch opening on one side (Figure 4).

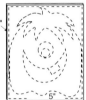

¼"

5"

Figure 4

7. Turn the stitched pillow right side out through the opening; poke out the corners and press flat at seams.

8. Insert the polyester fiberfill for desired loft.

9. Turn the opening edges to the inside ¼ inch and hand-stitch the opening closed to finish (Figure 5).

Figure 5

Friendly Monster Huggy Pillow
Placement Diagram 10" x 12", excluding arms

Friendly Monster Pillowcase

Finished Size
Pillowcase: Approximately 32¼ x 20¾ inches

Materials
- Cotton scraps
- Orange stripe
- Dark yellow tonal
- 1 fat quarter dark blue cotton polka dot
- 44/45-inch-wide cotton fabric:
    ¼ yard coordinating stripe
    ½ yard white solid
    ⅞ yard medium orange tonal
- Coordinating all-purpose thread
- Blue and green embroidery floss
- ¼ yard green jumbo rickrack
- ¼ yard 18-inch-wide double-stick fusible web
- Scrap white medium-weight fusible interfacing (optional)
- Basic sewing supplies and equipment

Cutting
Refer to General Instructions on page 3 for preparing and using patterns from page 51. Transfer all pattern markings to fabric. Use the Googly-Eyed Monster appliqué motif.

From orange stripe:
- Cut appliqué motif piece for Googly-Eyed Monster Nose.

From dark yellow tonal:
- Cut appliqué motif pieces for Googly-Eyed Monster Eyes.

From dark blue polka dot:
- Cut appliqué motif pieces for Googly-Eyed Monster Head and Fingers.

From coordinating stripe:
- Cut one 3 x 42-inch B strip.

From white solid:
- Cut one 12 x 42-inch C strip.

From medium orange tonal:
- Cut one 27 x 42-inch A strip.

Assembly
Stitch right sides together using a ¼-inch seam allowance unless otherwise specified. Refer to General Instructions on page 3 for Fusible Appliqué and Embroidery construction techniques.

1. Prepare the appliqué motif for the Googly-Eyed Monster.

2. Fold the C strip in half along length with wrong sides together to make a 6 x 42-inch; fold in half across width to make a four-layered 6 x 21-inch strip and press to form creases (Figure 1).

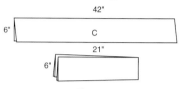

Figure 1

3. Unfold the C strip and lay flat with right side up. Center the appliqué motif within the creased lines on the top half of the left end of the strip and a scant ⅜ inch from the edge (Figure 2).

Figure 2

4. Cut two 3-inch lengths of green jumbo rickrack for antennae.

5. Tuck one end of each rickrack antenna under the top of the Head and pin to hold in place (Figure 3).

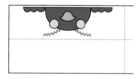

Figure 3

6. When satisfied with positioning of motif and rickrack, fuse in place.

7. Stitch appliqué pieces in place in numerical order using a machine blanket stitch and matching thread, sewing over ends of rickrack antennae when stitching Head; remove pins. Position rickrack antennae in a pleasing arc within the section and stitch down the center of each to hold in place.

8. Satin-stitch eyes using green embroidery floss.

9. Satin-stitch ¾-inch dots over the ends of rickrack antennae using using green embroidery floss referring to Figure 4 for positioning. Satin stitch eye irises as marked on pattern using blue embroidery floss, again referring to Figure 4.

Figure 4

10. Fold the B strip in half with wrong sides together along the length to make a double-layered 1½ x 42-inch strip.

11. Pin the folded B strip to one 42-inch edge of the A rectangle, matching raw edges; baste ⅛ inch from edge to hold in place (Figure 5). *Note: The folded edge of the B strip will be free from stitching and loose on top of A.*

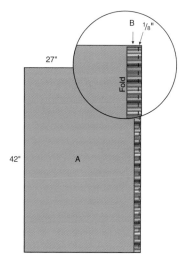

Figure 5

12. Fold under the long plain edge of C ¼ inch and press.

13. Place the C strip right sides together on top of the basted A-B unit, matching raw edges and stitch using a ¼-inch seam allowance (Figure 6).

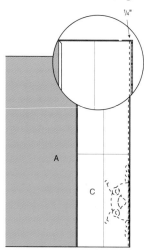

Figure 6

14. Press the C strip to the right side (Figure 7).

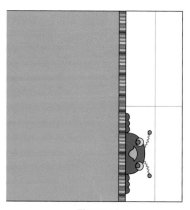

Figure 7

15. Turn the edge of the C strip to the inside along the previously creased line to cover and enclose the seam stitched in step 4; pin to hold (Figure 8).

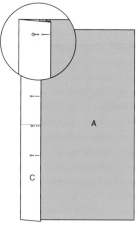

Figure 8

16. Topstitch on the B strip through all layers ⅛ inch from the A-B-C seam, catching the back-side folded edge of C in the stitching (Figure 9).

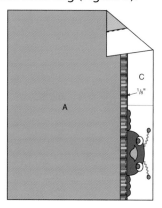

Figure 9

17. Fold the stitched section in half with right sides together, matching seams between A and B-C and keeping the folded B strip flat and pin to hold (Figure 10).

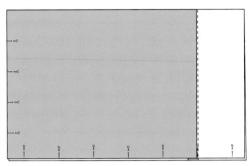

Figure 10

18. Stitch along the raw edge as pinned using a ¼-inch seam allowance. Serge or zigzag raw edges to secure. Turn right side out and press edges to finish.

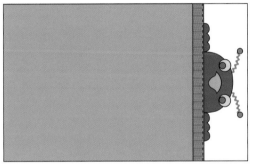

Friendly Monster Pillowcase
Placement Diagram Approximately 32¼" x 20¾"

Making a French Seam

If you prefer a stronger seam finish, instead of folding the stitched section right sides together as in step 8, fold it with wrong sides together and stitch. Then turn wrong side out and press. Fold again with right sides together and stitch a second seam ⅜ inch wide to enclose the first seam to make a French seam (Figure 11).

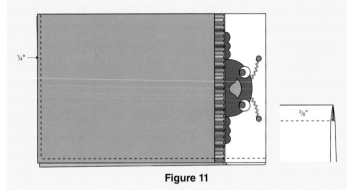

¼"

⅜"

Figure 11

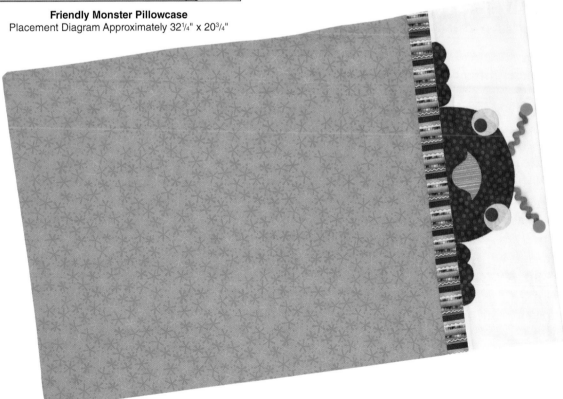

Adorable Animal Appliqué

Friendly Monster Wall Quilt

Finished Size
Wall Quilt: 30 x 38 inches

Materials
- Cotton scraps:
    Yellow/orange polka dot
    Yellow, medium green, dark green and medium blue tonals
- 1 fat quarter each cotton fabric:
    Green polka dot
    Light green and dark orange tonals
    Orange dot
    Dark blue print
- 44/45-inch-wide cotton fabric:
    ½ yard coordinating stripe
    ½ yard medium orange tonal
    ½ yard white solid
    ⅞ yard dark blue polka dot
- Coordinating all-purpose thread
- 1½ yards backing
- Batting 38 x 46 inches
- Blue, green and orange embroidery floss
- 7 inches blue medium rickrack
- 8 inches green narrow rickrack
- 9 inches ¼-inch-wide blue ribbon (for Blob Monster hair)
- 1 yard 18-inch-wide double-stick fusible web
- Scrap white medium-weight fusible interfacing (optional)
- Basic sewing supplies and equipment

Cutting
Refer to General Instructions on page 3 for preparing and using patterns. Transfer all pattern markings to fabric. Use the appliqué motifs for:

- Horned Monster—page 52
- Blob Monster—page 53
- One-Eyed Monster—page 54
- Frog Monster—page 55

From yellow/orange polka dot:
- Cut appliqué motif piece for Blob Monster Mouth.

From yellow tonal:
- Cut appliqué motif pieces for Frog Monster Mouth and Horned Monster Irises.

From medium green tonal:
- Cut appliqué motif pieces for One-Eyed Monster Ears.

From dark green tonal:
- Cut appliqué motif piece for One-Eyed Monster Tooth.

From medium blue tonal:
- Cut appliqué motif piece for Horned Monster Mouth.

From green polka dot:
- Cut appliqué motif pieces for One-Eyed Monster Iris and Frog Monster Body.

From light green tonal:
- Cut appliqué motif pieces for Blob Monster Left and Right Arms and Feet, and Horned Monster Hair.

From dark orange tonal:
- Cut appliqué motif piece for One-Eyed Monster Head.

From orange dot:
- Cut appliqué motif piece for Horned Monster Muzzle.

From dark blue print:
- Cut appliqué motif piece for Horned Monster Head.

From coordinating stripe:
- Cut appliqué motif pieces for Horned Monster Left and Right Horns.
- Cut four 2¼-inch by fabric width binding strips.

From medium orange tonal:
- Cut appliqué motif pieces for Blob Monster Horns.
- Cut four 2½-inch by fabric width strips. Subcut into two 2½ x 12½-inch B strips, one 2½ x 18½-inch C strip, two 2½ x 26½-inch D strips and two 2½ x 22½-inch E strips.

From white solid:
- Cut appliqué motif pieces for Frog Monster Eyes, One-Eyed Monster Eye, Horned Monster Eyes and Teeth, Blob Monster Eyes and Teeth.
- Cut one 12½-inch by fabric width strip. Subcut into four 8½ x 12½-inch A rectangles.

From dark blue polka dot:
- Cut appliqué motif piece for Blob Monster Body.
- Cut four 4½ x 30½-inch F strips.

From backing fabric:
- Cut one 38 x 46-inch backing rectangle.

Adorable Animal Appliqué

48

Assembly

Stitch right sides together using a ¼-inch seam allowance unless otherwise specified. Refer to General Instructions on page 3 for Fusible Appliqué, Embroidery, Quilting and Binding construction techniques.

1. Prepare the appliqué motifs for the Horned Monster, Blob Monster, Frog Monster and One-Eyed Monster.

2. Select the One-Eyed Monster motif. Pin the 7-inch length of blue medium rickrack in place for smile as marked on pattern for placement.

3. Cut two 3½-inch lengths green narrow rickrack for antennae.

4. Center and fuse the motif on one A rectangle, tucking the antennae under the Head as indicated on pattern (Figure 1).

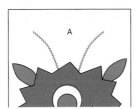

Figure 1

5. Stitch pieces in place in numerical order using a machine blanket stitch and matching thread.

6. Satin-stitch pupils using blue floss and dots at the ends of the green rickrack antennae using green floss, catching the ends of the rickrack in the stitching (Figure 2).

Figure 2

7. Cut blue ribbon into two equal-length pieces and repeat steps 4–6 with the Blob Monster motif, tucking ribbon under the Body motif as marked on pattern for placement (Figure 3) and using blue embroidery floss to satin-stitch irises. Stitch ribbon edges to the background.

Figure 3

8. Repeat steps 4–6 with Frog Monster and Horned Monster motifs using blue embroidery floss for pupils on the Horned Monster (Figure 4) and orange embroidery floss for the irises on the Frog Monster (Figure 5).

Figure 4

Figure 5

9. Join the One-Eyed Monster and Frog Monster with a B strip to make the top row (Figure 6); press.

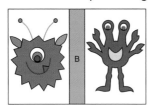

Figure 6

10. Join the Blob Monster and the Horned Monster with a B strip to make the bottom row (Figure 7); press.

Figure 7

11. Join the top and bottom rows with the C strip to complete the pieced center (Figure 8); press.

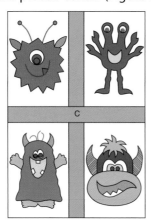

Figure 8

12. Sew a D strip to opposite sides and E strips to the top and bottom of the pieced center; press.

13. Sew F strips to opposite sides and then to the top and bottom of the pieced center to complete the wall quilt top; press.

14. Quilt as desired and bind to complete the Friendly Monster Wall Quilt. ■

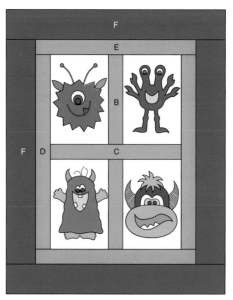

Friendly Monster Wall Quilt
Placement Diagram 30" x 38"

Using Appliqué Blocks

Each one of the appliquéd rectangles may be used to create other projects. The edges may be turned under all around and then appliquéd to the front or back sides of a tote. Any one of the designs may be used as a pillow front. If you join the rectangles side by side, you could make a bed scarf in the same manner as the Jungle Fun Bed Scarf on page 18.

Pattern Templates

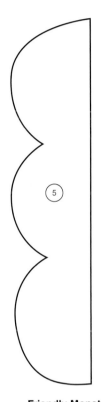

Friendly Monster Pillowcase
Fingers
Cut 2 dark blue polka dot

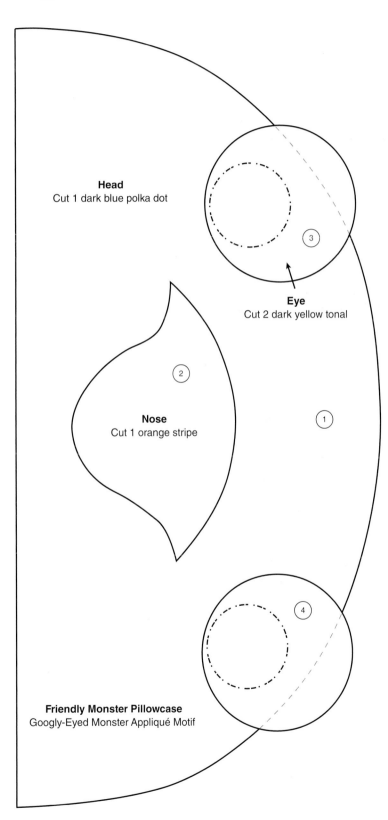

Head
Cut 1 dark blue polka dot

5

3

Eye
Cut 2 dark yellow tonal

2

Nose
Cut 1 orange stripe

1

4

Friendly Monster Pillowcase
Googly-Eyed Monster Appliqué Motif

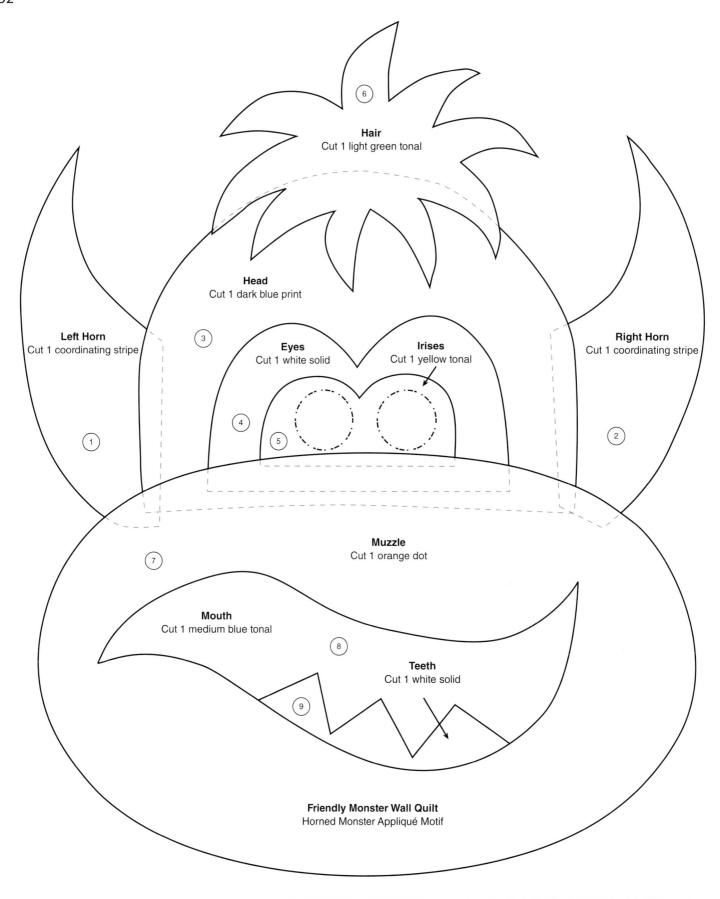

Hair
Cut 1 light green tonal

Head
Cut 1 dark blue print

Left Horn
Cut 1 coordinating stripe

Right Horn
Cut 1 coordinating stripe

Eyes
Cut 1 white solid

Irises
Cut 1 yellow tonal

Muzzle
Cut 1 orange dot

Mouth
Cut 1 medium blue tonal

Teeth
Cut 1 white solid

Friendly Monster Wall Quilt
Horned Monster Appliqué Motif

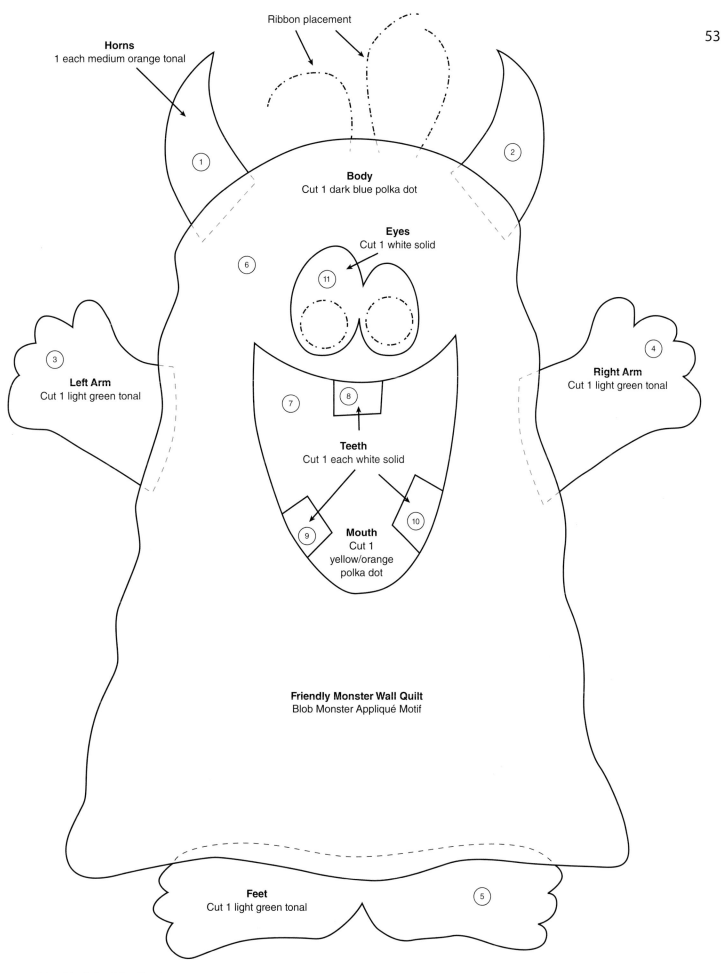

Ribbon placement

Horns
1 each medium orange tonal

Body
Cut 1 dark blue polka dot

Eyes
Cut 1 white solid

①

②

⑥

⑪

Left Arm
Cut 1 light green tonal

③

Right Arm
Cut 1 light green tonal

④

⑦

⑧

Teeth
Cut 1 each white solid

⑨

⑩

Mouth
Cut 1
yellow/orange
polka dot

Friendly Monster Wall Quilt
Blob Monster Appliqué Motif

Feet
Cut 1 light green tonal

⑤

Adorable Animal Appliqué

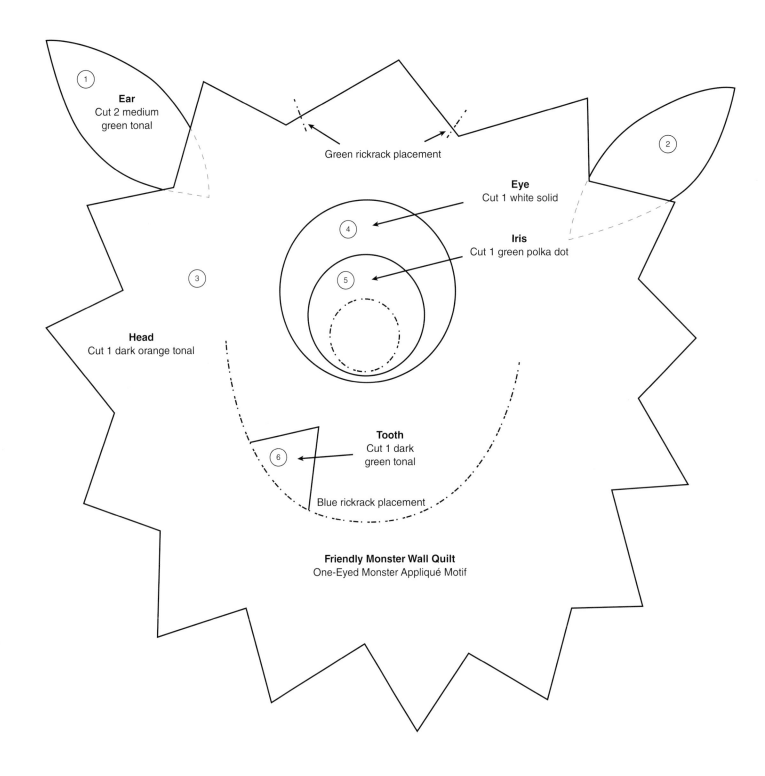

Ear
Cut 2 medium
green tonal

1

2

Green rickrack placement

Eye
Cut 1 white solid

4

Iris
Cut 1 green polka dot

5

3

Head
Cut 1 dark orange tonal

Tooth
Cut 1 dark
green tonal

6

Blue rickrack placement

Friendly Monster Wall Quilt
One-Eyed Monster Appliqué Motif

55

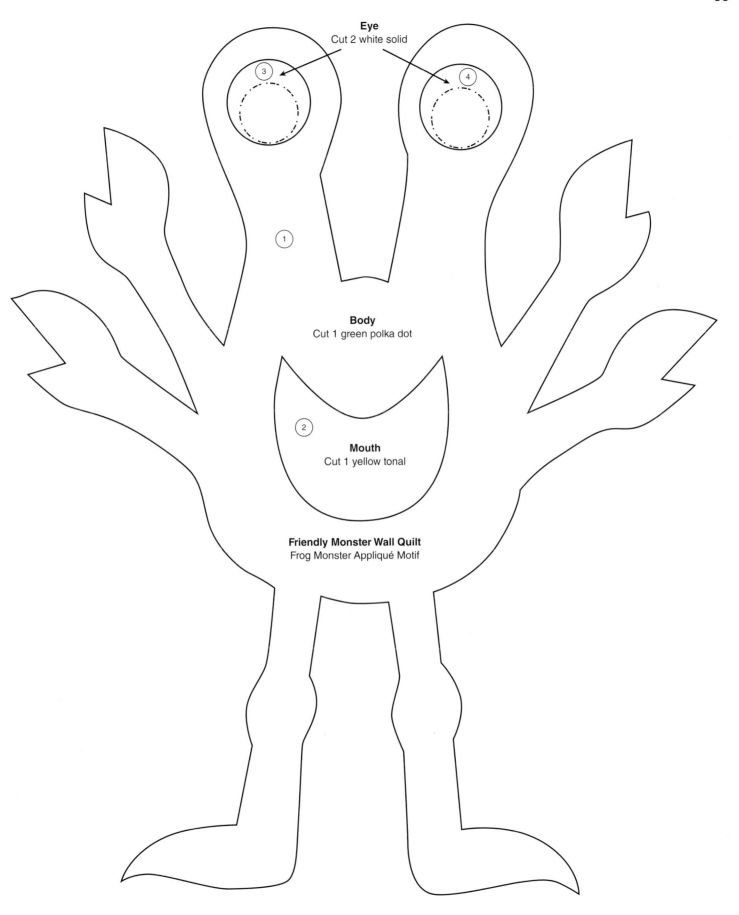

Eye
Cut 2 white solid

Body
Cut 1 green polka dot

Mouth
Cut 1 yellow tonal

Friendly Monster Wall Quilt
Frog Monster Appliqué Motif

Adorable Animal Appliqué

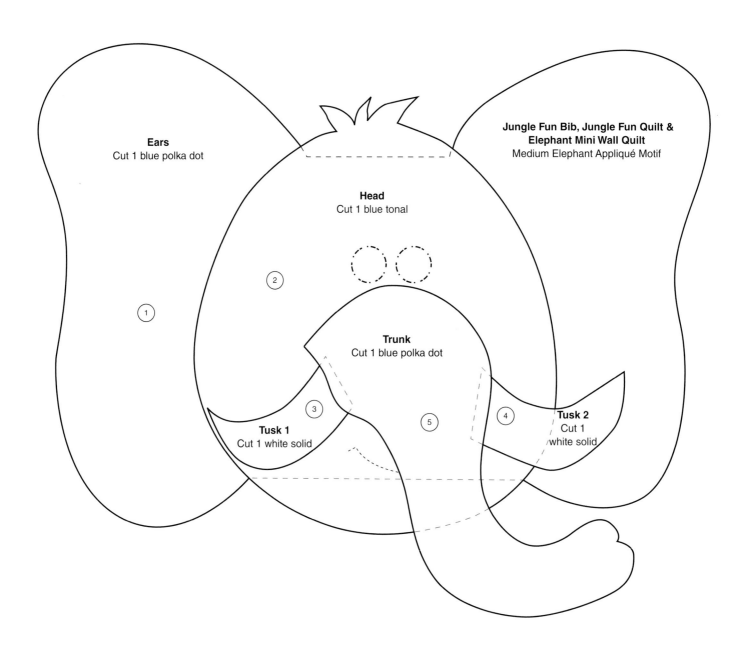

Ears
Cut 1 blue polka dot

Jungle Fun Bib, Jungle Fun Quilt &
Elephant Mini Wall Quilt
Medium Elephant Appliqué Motif

Head
Cut 1 blue tonal

Trunk
Cut 1 blue polka dot

Tusk 1
Cut 1 white solid

Tusk 2
Cut 1
white solid

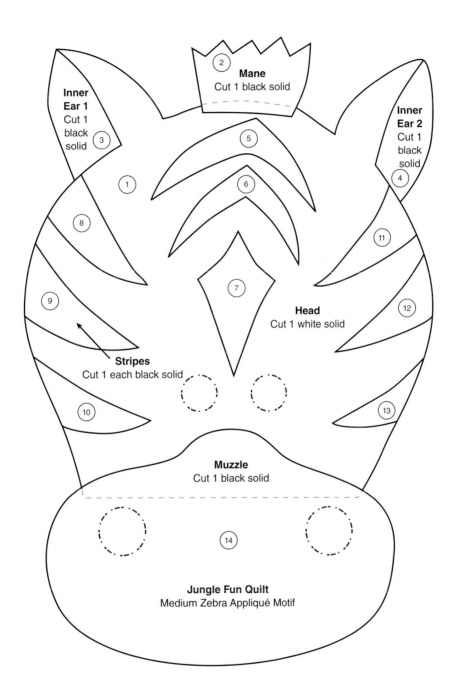

Mane
Cut 1 black solid

Inner Ear 1
Cut 1 black solid

Inner Ear 2
Cut 1 black solid

Head
Cut 1 white solid

Stripes
Cut 1 each black solid

Muzzle
Cut 1 black solid

Jungle Fun Quilt
Medium Zebra Appliqué Motif

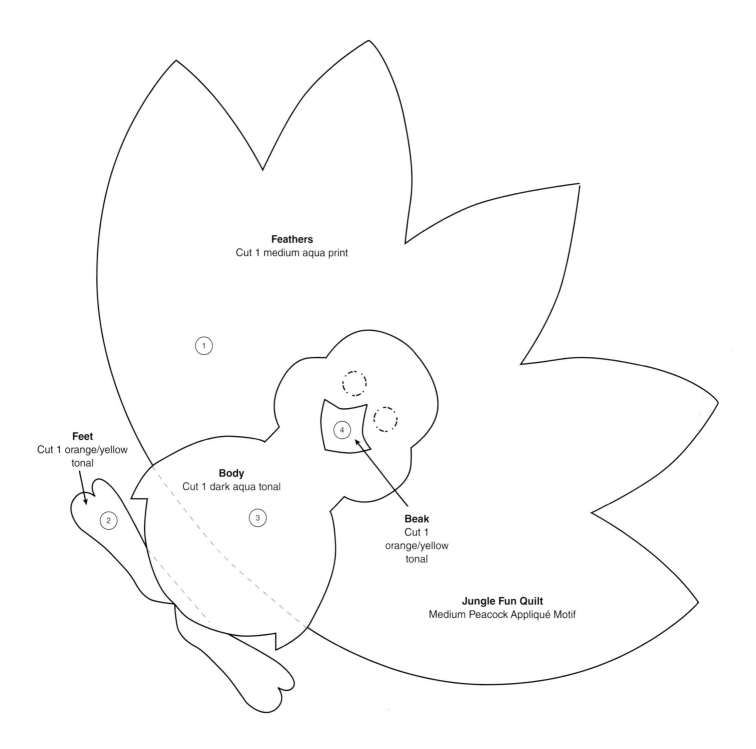

Feathers
Cut 1 medium aqua print

①

Feet
Cut 1 orange/yellow
tonal

②

Body
Cut 1 dark aqua tonal

③

④

Beak
Cut 1
orange/yellow
tonal

Jungle Fun Quilt
Medium Peacock Appliqué Motif

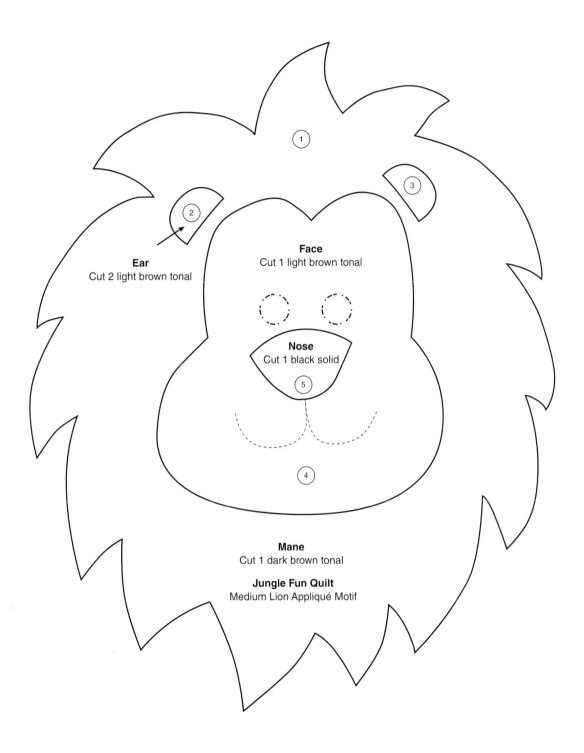

Ear
Cut 2 light brown tonal

Face
Cut 1 light brown tonal

Nose
Cut 1 black solid

Mane
Cut 1 dark brown tonal

Jungle Fun Quilt
Medium Lion Appliqué Motif

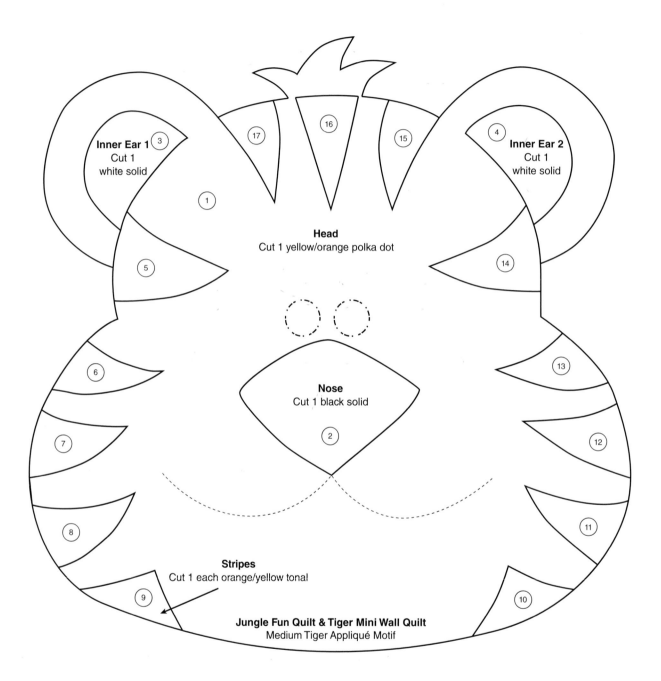

Inner Ear 1
Cut 1
white solid

Inner Ear 2
Cut 1
white solid

Head
Cut 1 yellow/orange polka dot

Nose
Cut 1 black solid

Stripes
Cut 1 each orange/yellow tonal

Jungle Fun Quilt & Tiger Mini Wall Quilt
Medium Tiger Appliqué Motif

61

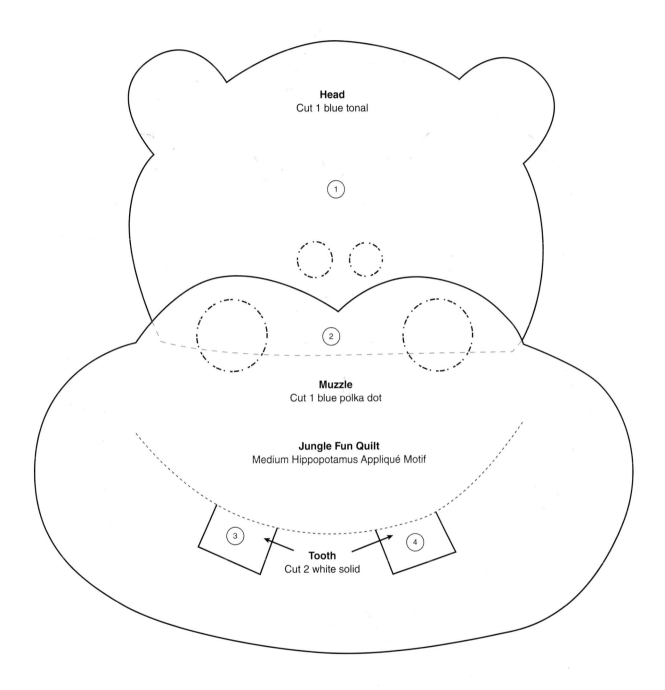

Head
Cut 1 blue tonal

1

Muzzle
Cut 1 blue polka dot

2

Jungle Fun Quilt
Medium Hippopotamus Appliqué Motif

3

Tooth
Cut 2 white solid

4

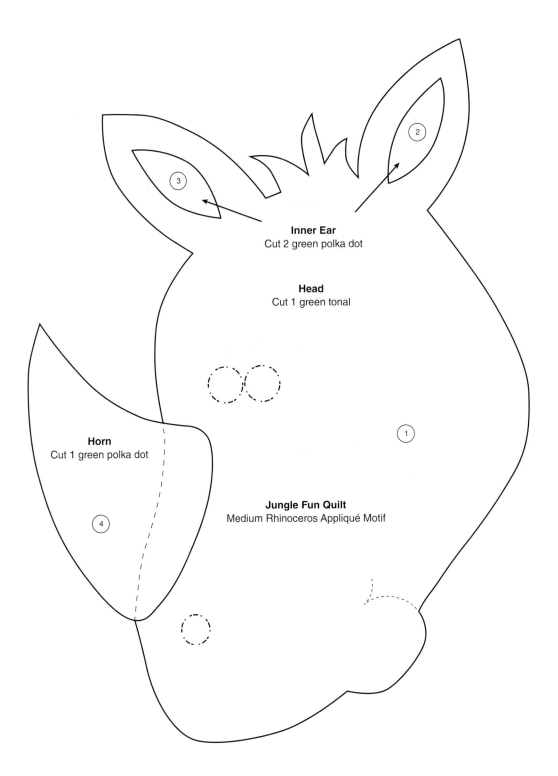

Inner Ear
Cut 2 green polka dot

Head
Cut 1 green tonal

Horn
Cut 1 green polka dot

Jungle Fun Quilt
Medium Rhinoceros Appliqué Motif

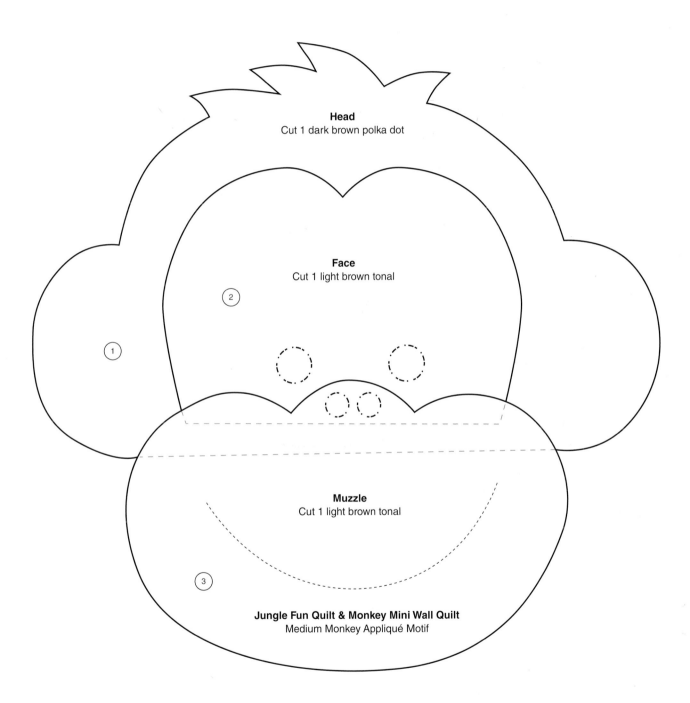

Head
Cut 1 dark brown polka dot

Face
Cut 1 light brown tonal

2

1

Muzzle
Cut 1 light brown tonal

3

Jungle Fun Quilt & Monkey Mini Wall Quilt
Medium Monkey Appliqué Motif

Adorable Animal Appliqué

Special Thanks

All projects were quilted by Brandy Mascher.

We would like to thank the following manufacturers who provided materials to our designer to make sample projects for this book.

Jungle Animal Set, pages 6–25: Zoofari Organic by Doodlebug Designs and Cotton Shade fabric collections from Riley Blake (www.rileyblakedesigns.com); Cuddle low-pile, smooth fleece from Shannon Fabrics (www.shannonfabrics.com); Lite Steam-A-Seam 2 double-stick fusible web from The Warm Company (www.warmcompany.com); 50 wt. cotton thread from Aurifil (www.aurifil.com).

Under the Sea Set, pages 26–35: Batiks from Timeless Treasures (www.ttfabrics.com); Cuddle low-pile, smooth fleece from Shannon Fabrics (www.shannonfabrics.com); Lite Steam-A-Seam 2 double-stick fusible web from The Warm Company (www.warmcompany.com); 50 wt. cotton thread from Aurifil (www.aurifil.com).

Friendly Monster Set, pages 36–50: Cuddle low-pile, smooth fleece from Shannon Fabrics (www.shannonfabrics.com); Lite Steam-A-Seam 2 double-stick fusible web from The Warm Company (www.warmcompany.com); 50 wt. cotton thread from Aurifil (www.aurifil.com).

Photo Index

6

26

36

ISBN: 978-1-59635-722-8

1 2 3 4 5 6 7 8 9